Forecasting Disasters

TSUNAMIS

Trudy Becker

WWW.APEXEDITIONS.COM

Copyright © 2026 by Apex Editions, Mendota Heights, MN 55120. All rights reserved. No part of this book may be reproduced or utilized in any form or by any means without written permission from the publisher.

Apex is distributed by North Star Editions:
sales@northstareditions.com | 888-417-0195

Produced for Apex by Red Line Editorial.

Photographs ©: Kyodo News/AP Images, cover, 1; Shutterstock Images, 4–5, 6–7, 8–9, 14–15, 16–17, 18–19, 20–21, 24–25, 36–37, 41, 42–43, 48–49, 52–53, 54–55, 58; David Rydevik/Wikimedia Commons, 10–11; Noah Berger/AP Images, 12–13; North Wind Picture Archives/Alamy, 22–23; Ronen Zilberman/AP Images, 26–27; Patrick M. Bonafede/US Navy/Getty Images News/Getty Images, 29; US Geological Survey, 30–31, 32–33; Allen Shimada/National Oceanic and Atmospheric Administration, 34–35; Al Grillo/AP Images, 38–39; NOAA Center for Tsunami Research/Getty Images News/Getty Images, 44–45; Marcos Reategui/Getty Images News/Getty Images, 46–47; Ben Smegelsky/NASA, 50–51; John De Mello/Alamy, 56–57

Library of Congress Control Number: 2025930908

ISBN
979-8-89250-664-9 (hardcover)
979-8-89250-699-1 (ebook pdf)
979-8-89250-682-3 (hosted ebook)

Printed in the United States of America
Mankato, MN
082025

NOTE TO PARENTS AND EDUCATORS

Apex books are designed to build literacy skills in striving readers. Exciting, high-interest content attracts and holds readers' attention. The text is carefully leveled to allow students to achieve success quickly.

TABLE OF CONTENTS

Chapter 1

WILD WAVES 5

Chapter 2

WHAT ARE TSUNAMIS? 10

Chapter 3

EARLY TSUNAMI FORECASTING 20

That's Wild!

INDIAN OCEAN TSUNAMI 28

Chapter 4

MODERN METHODS 30

That's Wild!

DISASTER IN JAPAN 40

Chapter 5

MODELING TSUNAMIS 43

Chapter 6

FUTURE FORECASTING 50

TIMELINE • 59
COMPREHENSION QUESTIONS • 60
GLOSSARY • 62
TO LEARN MORE • 63
ABOUT THE AUTHOR • 63
INDEX • 64

Talise Beach is in the city of Palu, Indonesia.

Chapter 1

WILD WAVES

It's September 2018. Swimmers splash in the water at Talise Beach in Indonesia. Other beachgoers sunbathe on the sand. Suddenly, the ground begins to shake. An earthquake has hit the area.

A few moments later, the shaking stops. It seems like the danger is gone. But far out at sea, water is moving fast. Giant waves rise out of the ocean. They grow taller and taller as they hurtle toward shore.

In 2018, Indonesia had nine large earthquakes.

More than 210,000 people had to leave their homes after the Palu tsunami.

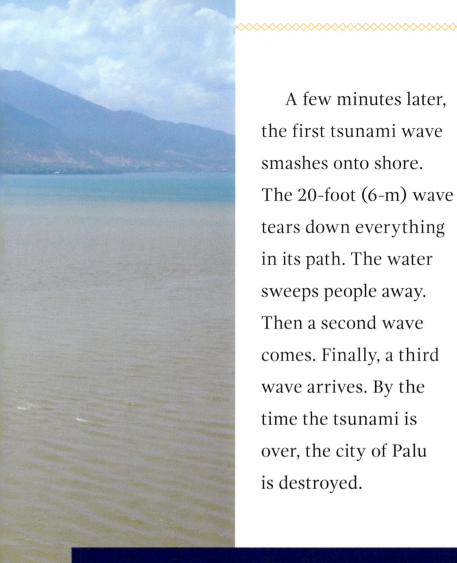

A few minutes later, the first tsunami wave smashes onto shore. The 20-foot (6-m) wave tears down everything in its path. The water sweeps people away. Then a second wave comes. Finally, a third wave arrives. By the time the tsunami is over, the city of Palu is destroyed.

NOT ENOUGH WARNING

The 2018 earthquake set off a tsunami warning. But the local sirens never went off. The earthquake had cut off their power. The earthquake took down cell-phone towers, too. So, text-message alerts did not go out. People had no time to get to safety. Thousands died.

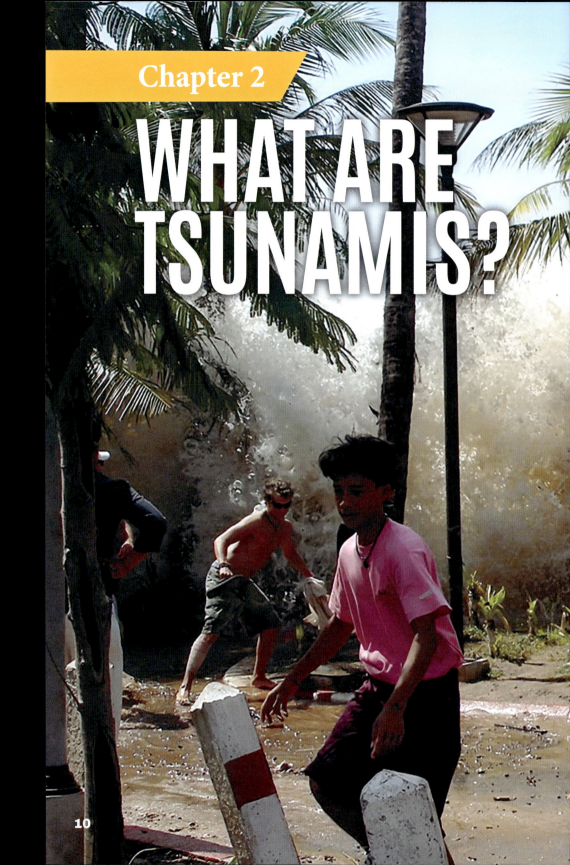

Chapter 2
WHAT ARE TSUNAMIS?

Tsunamis are giant sets of waves. The disasters are usually caused by earthquakes under the sea. Tsunami waves can be more than 100 feet (30 m) tall. They can stretch nearly 100 miles (160 km) wide.

People sometimes call tsunamis "tidal waves." However, tsunamis are not related to tides.

During an earthquake, Earth's tectonic plates shift. When that happens underwater, the movement shoves water upward. That creates massive waves. They move fast at first. As the waves move closer to shore, they slow down. But they also grow taller.

JAPANESE TO ENGLISH

The word *tsunami* is Japanese. *Tsu* means "harbor." A harbor is an area of water near shore where boats tie up. *Nami* means "wave." Over time, English speakers started using the word *tsunami*, too.

Tsunami waves can travel 500 miles per hour (805 km/h) at sea.

The Ring of Fire runs about 25,000 miles (40,200 km).

Most tsunamis happen in the Pacific Ocean. In that area, volcanic eruptions often shift the ground. So, countries along the Pacific face more tsunamis than anywhere else. Japan and Indonesia are two examples. Russia, Chile, and the United States see many tsunamis, too.

RING OF FIRE

The Ring of Fire is in the Pacific Ocean. This area includes more than 450 volcanos. That makes volcanic eruptions and earthquakes common. About 80 percent of tsunamis happen in the Ring of Fire.

Tsunami damage is extreme. The strong waves tear down buildings. They destroy power lines. They block roads and flood farms. Waves toss dangerous debris, too. The destruction is costly. Tsunami damage can cost billions of dollars to fix.

LOSING WHOLE TOWNS

In 1868, a huge earthquake shook the southern Pacific Ocean. It caused a tsunami. The tsunami smashed onto shore in several countries. Huge waves wiped away entire coastal towns in Peru and Chile.

Floods caused by tsunamis can cover houses.

Tsunamis are deadly. Drowning is the biggest risk. It causes about 90 percent of tsunami deaths. People often get trapped underwater. In some cases, waves sweep people out to sea. Falling pieces of buildings hurt people, too. So do bits of debris in the rushing water.

UNSAFE WATER

Some tsunamis destroy water treatment plants. They can break sewer pipes, too. The flowing water contains pollution. People have no way to get clean water. So, people may get sick from the water.

Dirty water often causes diseases such as cholera and typhoid.

Chapter 3

EARLY TSUNAMI FORECASTING

Scientists can track some storms. For example, forecasters spot hurricanes days ahead of time. They watch as the storms get closer. Tsunamis are different. They appear suddenly. But over time, people noticed a pattern. They learned that tsunamis arrived after earthquakes.

In Ancient Greece, some people thought the god of the sea caused tsunamis when he was angry.

People in the past found ways to get ready for tsunamis. In Japan, people ran to higher ground when they felt the ground shake. However, in most cases, people could not prepare. They had to fix things after tsunamis. In some areas, people rebuilt ovens first. That way, tsunami victims could eat.

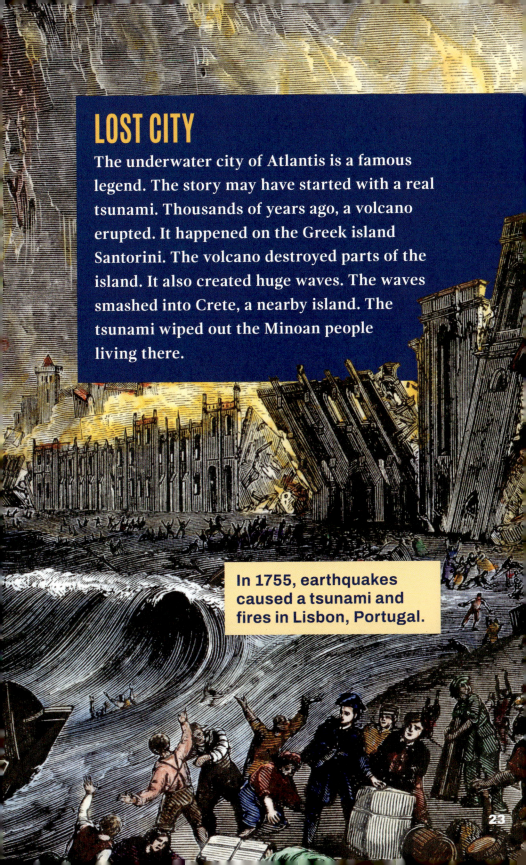

LOST CITY

The underwater city of Atlantis is a famous legend. The story may have started with a real tsunami. Thousands of years ago, a volcano erupted. It happened on the Greek island Santorini. The volcano destroyed parts of the island. It also created huge waves. The waves smashed into Crete, a nearby island. The tsunami wiped out the Minoan people living there.

In 1755, earthquakes caused a tsunami and fires in Lisbon, Portugal.

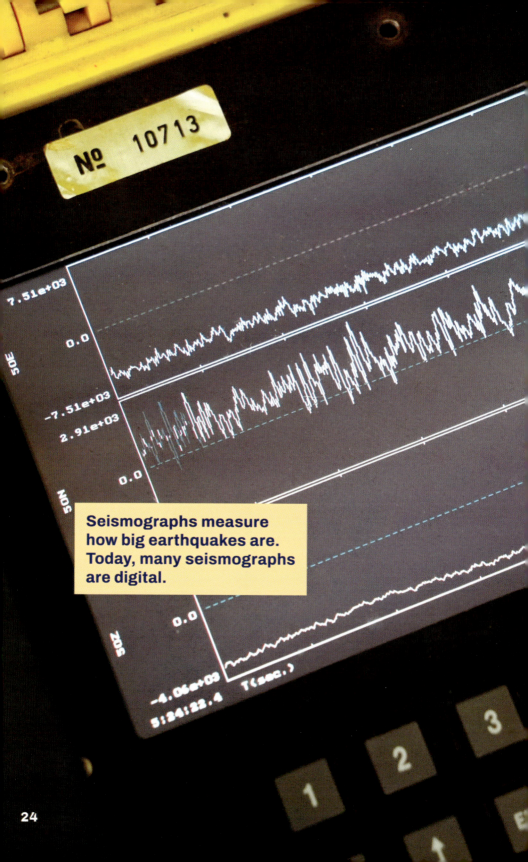

Seismographs measure how big earthquakes are. Today, many seismographs are digital.

24

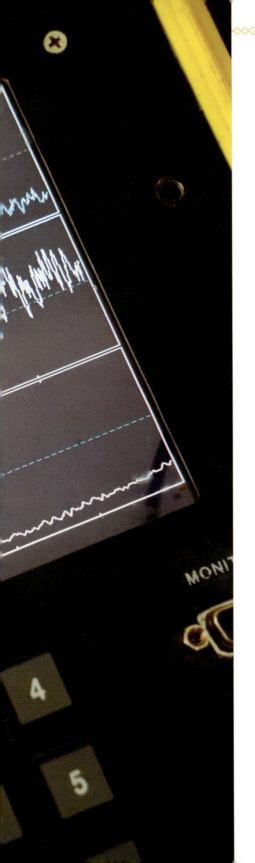

People have measured seismic activity for hundreds of years. Seismic tools record how much the ground shakes during earthquakes. By the 1900s, scientists were using these tools to forecast tsunamis. The seismic waves tell scientists an earthquake's location. They show its size, too. From that information, scientists made guesses. A bigger earthquake could mean a bigger tsunami was coming.

25

As the 1900s went on, people built tsunami warning centers. These stations sat near water. They had many seismic tools. People often created new stations after disasters. For example, a huge tsunami hit Hawaiʻi in 1946. Then, in 1949, a new warning center opened there. All the warning centers collected tsunami information.

HOLDING HISTORY

Trees can hold records of past tsunamis. Their wood shows signs of saltwater flooding. Trunk markings help, too. The rings show when trees grew slowly. Modern scientists learn from the trees. They study the effects of past disasters. That helps them guess the effects of future tsunamis.

The National Weather Service has two tsunami warning centers. People work there 24 hours a day.

That's Wild!

INDIAN OCEAN TSUNAMI

In 2004, a massive earthquake shook the Indian Ocean. Tsunami waves rocked several countries. Many people had no time to escape. More than 230,000 people lost their lives. It was the deadliest tsunami in history.

Forecasters had sent out warnings before the waves hit. But the alerts were too slow. And they didn't reach enough people. Later, people built new warning centers. They aimed to be better prepared next time.

The earthquake that caused the 2004 tsunami happened about 18 miles (29 km) below the ocean's floor.

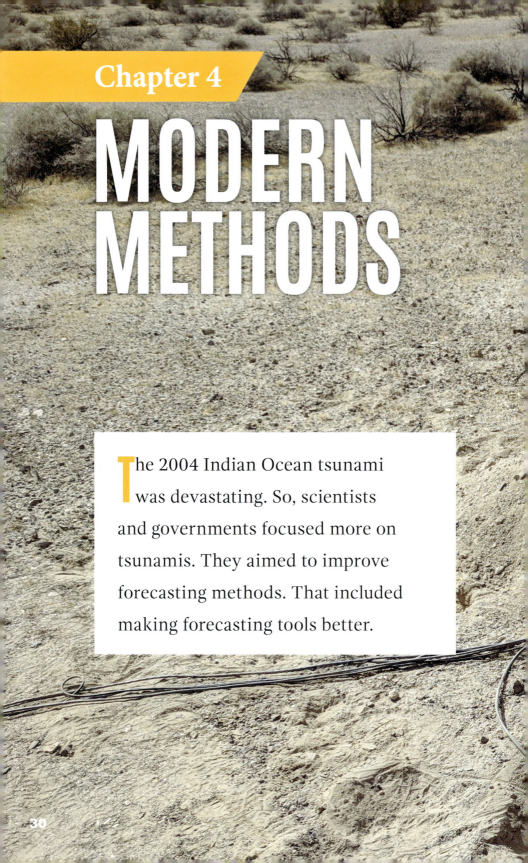

Chapter 4
MODERN METHODS

The 2004 Indian Ocean tsunami was devastating. So, scientists and governments focused more on tsunamis. They aimed to improve forecasting methods. That included making forecasting tools better.

Scientists can use portable sensors to measure earthquakes from different places.

In the 2000s, scientists improved seismic tools. The changes made measurements more accurate. People also created new ways to use those tools. For example, most early seismic tools sat on land. New ones can work underwater. Scientists place them directly on the seafloor. That way, scientists get information about underwater earthquakes more quickly.

Some seismic stations house their tools in towers.

Measuring devices on DART buoys are at least 9,800 feet (3,000 m) deep.

DART buoys are an important modern tool. DART stands for Deep ocean Assessment and Reporting of Tsunamis. DART buoys float on the water. Scientists place them near fault lines. Earthquakes are more likely to happen there. The buoys are linked to devices on the ocean floor. Every 15 seconds, the devices take measurements. They track water pressure and temperature. Tsunami warning centers get the information.

DROPPING DARTs

DART buoys are easy to place. First, ships carry the buoys out to sea. Then people dump the DARTs into the water. The buoys right themselves. They float. Then the buoys let down anchors. The anchors include measuring devices.

Sometimes, water levels drop before a tsunami hits.

Modern tsunami forecasters use other tools, too. For example, water level is a key measurement. Changes in water level can show if waves are approaching or forming.

Some water-level devices sit on shore. They look out toward sea and take pictures. Other devices go into the water. The tools measure the water level every few minutes.

Water-level data and DART information go to tsunami warning centers. Today, warning centers around the world work together. They quickly collect information in their area. Then they share it. That helps teams around the world make better forecasts.

By the mid-2020s, there were about 1,400 tsunami warning centers around the world.

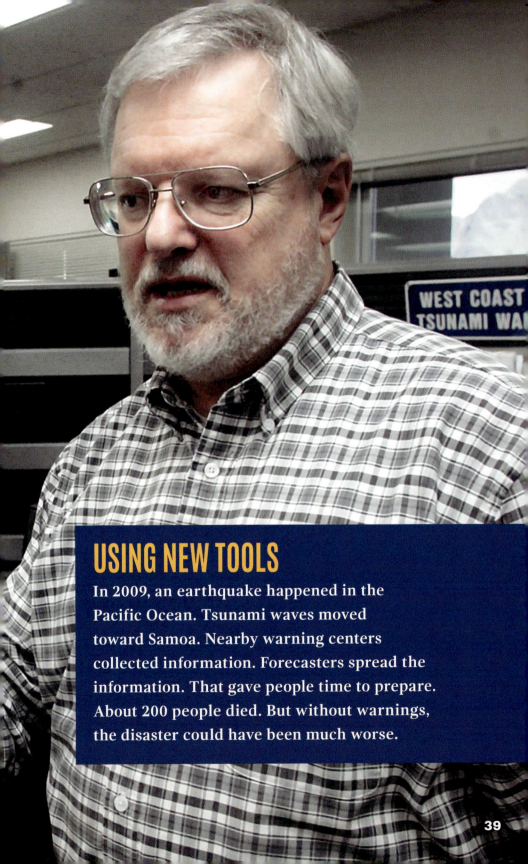

USING NEW TOOLS

In 2009, an earthquake happened in the Pacific Ocean. Tsunami waves moved toward Samoa. Nearby warning centers collected information. Forecasters spread the information. That gave people time to prepare. About 200 people died. But without warnings, the disaster could have been much worse.

That's Wild!

DISASTER IN JAPAN

In 2011, an earthquake caused a tsunami in Japan. Huge waves smashed the coast. More than 15,000 people died.

The tsunami caused a second disaster. In Fukushima, a nuclear power plant lost power. That caused the plant to overheat. As a result, part of the plant melted down. Dangerous radiation spread. Many people had to leave the area.

The tsunami's cost was huge. It caused more than $300 billion in damage.

More than 300,000 people had to leave Fukushima after the tsunami and nuclear disaster.

```python
    def __repr__(self):
        return '<Task %r>' % self.id


@app.route('/', methods=['POST', 'GET'])
def index():
    if request.method == 'POST':
        task_content = request.form['content']
        new_task = Todo(content=task_content)

        try:
            if task_content == True:
                task_content.

            db.session.add(new_task)
            db.session.commit()
            return redirect('/')
        except:
            return 'There was an issue adding your task'

    else:
        tasks = Todo.query.order_by(Todo.date_created).all()
        return render_template('index.html', tasks=tasks)


@app.route('/delete/<int:id>')
def delete(id):
    task_to_delete = Todo.query.get_or_404(id)

    try:
        db.session.delete(task_to_delete)
        db.session.commit()
        return redirect('/')
    except:
```

Computer models can create predictions much faster than people can.

Chapter 5

MODELING TSUNAMIS

Computers models are another essential forecasting tool. Computer models are made of code. The coded programs create predictions for forecasters to use.

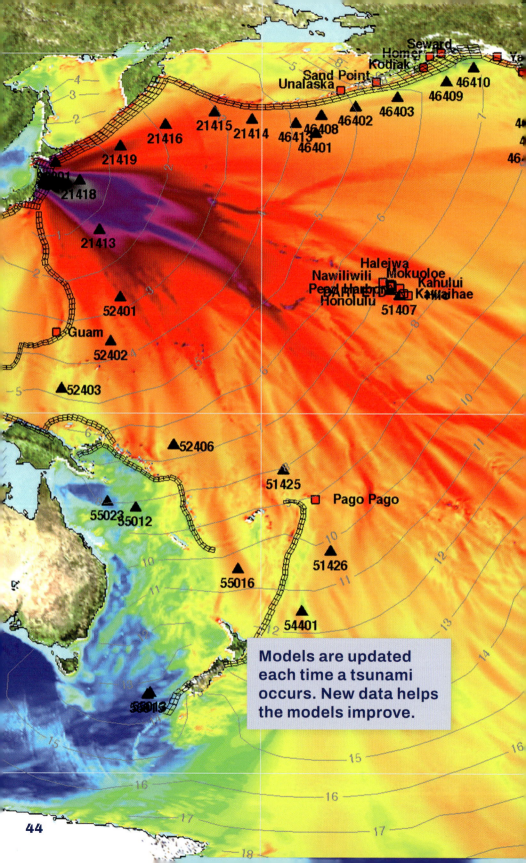

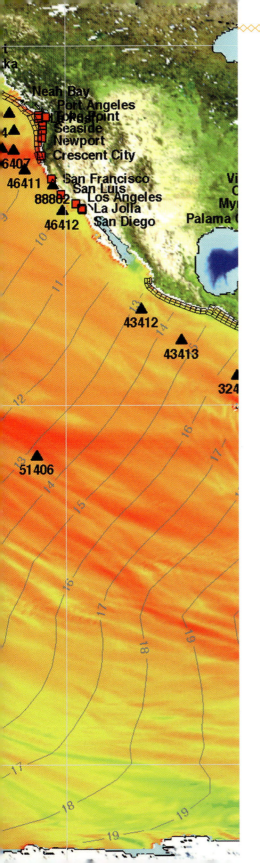

Tsunami computer models need lots of data. The information comes from many sources. People put data from DART buoys into tsunami models. The models use water-level data, too. They also include information about nearby land. For example, people enter the sizes of nearby mountains or harbors. The programs include historical data, too. They use information from past tsunamis.

45

When an earthquake hits, the program puts together all that data. It comes up with a specific prediction for what may happen. The model guesses the tsunami's speed. It says where the waves will hit. The model predicts when the tsunami will arrive, too.

UNDERWATER VOLCANO

In 2022, an underwater volcano erupted. It shook waters in the Pacific Ocean. Tsunami waves hurtled toward several countries. But scientists had measured the volcano's progress. When it erupted, forecasters worked quickly. They warned nearby people to move away from beaches. People found higher ground. Only a few people died.

In Peru, large waves from a 2022 eruption hit a ship. The ship spilled large amounts of oil.

47

After models make predictions, forecasters spread the word. Radio and TV stations share details. Loud sirens blare alerts. Most countries also use newer, high-tech systems. For example, people get alert messages on their phones. Modern forecasting makes the whole process fast. People can get alerts just five minutes after an earthquake hits.

GOOD ALERTS

A useful tsunami alert does two main things. First, the alert gives people key details. It states when a tsunami is coming. And it says where the tsunami will hit. Second, the alert tells people what to do. For example, alerts often tell people to move away from shore.

Places near oceans may show warning signs for tsunamis.

Chapter 6

FUTURE FORECASTING

Scientists are still working to improve tsunami forecasts. For example, people have started using satellites in new ways. Some satellites measure water levels from above. Others keep track of changes in the air. Both measures can show the size and movement of tsunamis.

NASA and weather organizations work together to create weather satellites.

Typhoons are hurricanes that start near Japan, China, or Southeast Asia.

Other scientists are using artificial intelligence (AI) to forecast tsunamis. AI models analyze earthquake data. Many AI models are superfast. They can make tsunami predictions in less than a second. Forecasters can use the predictions alongside other models. That helps them make good guesses.

AI FOR WEATHER

Forecasters use AI to predict several types of storms. Scientists can use it for blizzards and hurricanes. In 2024, forecasters in Taiwan used AI models. The models helped people prepare for a typhoon.

53

Drones are another forecasting tool. Some drones film water-level changes from above. Others can help people during disasters. For example, drones can blast loud alarms. People can hear these sirens even if the power goes out. Drones can also fly through dangerous areas. They can spot people who need to be saved.

When a tsunami happens, getting information out quickly is important.

Wave Gliders can patrol 24 hours a day.

Scientists also use robots for tsunami forecasts. Wave Glider is one example. The Wave Glider robot floats on the surface of the ocean. It sends back information from deep-sea tools. Robots can also watch volcanos. If an eruption could cause a tsunami, the robot can spread the word.

ENERGY

Tsunami robots can run on gasoline. But they can also gather energy from the ocean's movement. They can use energy from the sun, too. These sources power the robots for a long time. Some float for a year before needing more fuel.

TIMELINE

1868 — Tsunami waves wipe out coastal towns in Peru and Chile.

1949 — A new tsunami warning center is built in Hawai'i after a tsunami hit there three years earlier.

2004 — The deadliest tsunami in history hits countries along the Indian Ocean.

2009 — Many people in Samoa are prepared for a tsunami thanks to early warnings.

2011 — An earthquake and tsunami knock out power at a nuclear power plant in Japan.

2018 — A tsunami kills many beachgoers in Palu, Indonesia.

2022 — Good forecasts help people prepare after an underwater volcanic explosion causes a tsunami in the Pacific Ocean.

COMPREHENSION QUESTIONS

Write your answers on a separate piece of paper.

1. Write a few sentences describing the main points of Chapter 2.

2. Which tool do you think is most helpful for forecasting tsunamis? Why?

3. When did the deadliest tsunami in history strike the Indian Ocean?
   A. 1868
   B. 2004
   C. 2011

4. After a tsunami, how can drones help?
   A. Drones can find people who need to be rescued.
   B. Drones can dive underwater and save people who are drowning.
   C. Drones are only used before tsunamis hit.

5. What does **pollution** mean in this book?

*Some tsunamis destroy water treatment plants. They can break sewer pipes, too. The flowing water contains **pollution**. People have no way to get clean water.*

    A. dirty things
    B. clean things
    C. broken things

6. What does **essential** mean in this book?

*Computers models are another **essential** forecasting tool. Computer models are made of code. The coded programs create predictions for forecasters to use.*

    A. confusing
    B. useless
    C. important

Answer key on page 64.

GLOSSARY

artificial intelligence
Computer systems that can learn and change without following new instructions.

buoys
Floating objects anchored in the sea.

code
Instructions that tell a computer or device what to do.

debris
Pieces of something that broke or fell apart.

drones
Aircraft that people control from far away or that work on their own.

nuclear power plant
A place that makes energy by splitting tiny bits of matter called atoms.

radiation
Energy given off by tiny, fast-moving bits of matter. In some cases, this energy can be harmful.

satellites
Devices that orbit Earth, often to send or collect information.

seismic activity
Movement of Earth's crust, often related to earthquakes.

tectonic plates
Massive pieces of rock that make up Earth's crust.

TO LEARN MORE

BOOKS

Adamson, Thomas K. *The Indian Ocean Tsunami*.
  Bellwether Media, 2022.
Becker, Trudy. *Floods*. Apex Editions, 2026.
Spilsbury, Louise. *The Science Behind Mega
  Tsunamis*. Lerner Publications, 2022.

ONLINE RESOURCES

Visit **www.apexeditions.com** to find links and
resources related to this title.

ABOUT THE AUTHOR

Trudy Becker lives in Minneapolis, Minnesota.
She likes exploring new places and loves anything
involving books.

INDEX

alerts, 9, 28, 48
artificial intelligence (AI), 53
Atlantis, 23

Chile, 15–16
computer models, 43, 45–46, 48, 53

debris, 16, 18
Deep ocean Assessment and Reporting of Tsunamis (DART), 35, 38, 45
drones, 54

earthquakes, 5–6, 9, 11–12, 15–16, 20, 22, 25, 28, 32, 35, 39, 40, 46, 48, 53

forecasting, 20, 25, 28, 30, 37–39, 43, 46, 48, 50, 53–54, 57
Fukushima, 40

Indonesia, 5–7, 15

Japan, 13, 15, 22, 40

measuring, 25, 32, 35, 37, 46, 50

Pacific Ocean, 15–16, 39, 46

Ring of Fire, 15
Russia, 15

satellites, 50
scientists, 25, 27, 30, 32, 35, 46, 53, 57
seismic tools, 25–26, 32

tectonic plates, 12
tsunami warning centers, 26, 28, 35, 38–39

volcanoes, 15, 23, 46, 57

water-level data, 37–38, 45, 54
Wave Glider, 57
waves, 6, 9, 11–13, 16, 18, 23, 25, 28, 37, 39, 40, 46

ANSWER KEY:

1. Answers will vary; 2. Answers will vary; 3. B; 4. A; 5. A; 6. C